The Power of Halloween

The Power of Halloween

Diana Millay

iUniverse, Inc.
New York Lincoln Shanghai

The Power of Halloween

iUniverse, Inc.

For information address:
iUniverse, Inc.
2021 Pine Lake Road, Suite 100
Lincoln, NE 68512
www.iuniverse.com

ISBN: 0-595-29263-1

Printed in the United States of America

For my son,

Kiley Jones,

in the hope that someday

he might read this

and better understand

his unusual and gifted ancestors.

"For Those Who Believe,
No Words Are Necessary.
For Those Who Do Not Believe,
No Words Are Possible."
                              —*St. Ignatius Loyola*

Contents

Part II: Halloween's Legacy

Acknowledgements

I am very grateful to my ancestors for having lived lives worth writing about in times worth remembering. They were witches—miracle makers—and I am thankful for their wisdom and indebted to them for channeling that and much more to me.

My appreciation to the living for their inspiration and undying passion to learn more about a holiday that was born at the beginning of time and will live to the end of it.

Most especially, many thanks to my editor, Craig Hamrick, who suggested I write this book and then refused to take no for an answer. This is not our first collaboration. Whatever I put on paper, Craig somehow manages to decipher my thinking and edit my writing. I am forever in his debt.

Foreword

As a consulting editor, I've worked for many clients in New York City and throughout the country. In late 2002 I found myself at Martha Stewart Living Omnimedia, helping edit Martha's holiday catalog. It was a busy assignment, but whenever I had a free moment, I thumbed through the library of various publications the domestic doyenne had written over the years: books and magazines about arts & crafts and entertaining, including an interesting volume about how to celebrate Halloween.

Inspiration struck. Diana Millay and I had recently discussed her next book, trying to determine what subject she should explore, but we hadn't settled on one. Now it occurred to me that Diana's core audience would be interested in her tips on how to celebrate a spooky Halloween.

I had something "very Martha" in mind, and I quickly sketched an outline including how-to items, like directions for creating party favors, recipes for ghoulish delights, and suggestions about hosting the perfect haunted Halloween bash.

Diana loved the concept. She was ready to start right away. However, much to my surprise, she took that spark and went in a completely different direction. While the resulting book does end with party tips and recipes, the bulk of it explores Halloween's mysteries and magic. It's a journey into a mystical realm where life is surrounded by good and evil, ghosts and goblins, saints and sinners.

—Craig Hamrick
August 2003

PART I

Halloween:
Mysteries & Magic

1

In the Beginning

Have you ever wondered about the true meaning of Halloween? It's great fun for kids but after the tricks and treats…where do the adults fit in?

Halloween may be the most misunderstood holiday on the calendar, because we don't realize the depth of its history. Nor do we realize its power and its purpose, which benefit all of mankind—those who are with us now, and those who have moved into the hereafter.

Over the centuries, Halloween has become a mixture of its many masters. For without realizing it, these untamed conquerors lifted a "cloud of unknowing" from the hearts and minds of man. Grief turned to relief when there was no longer a need to ask, is this life all there is?

The answer to this and many more questions was found within the rituals of Halloween. It was the frequent repetition of them, not just on Halloween, that cleared a path to something more. Always available but undiscovered, answers slowly came to light in the minds of man through the power of Halloween and the power of witches.

While there are still a few "clouds" hanging over life today, it is my hope that more answers will fall from confusion into understanding as pages are turned.

This once-sacred holiday has, over time, evolved from a night of merry-making and mischief to a much more sinister atmosphere of yesteryear inhabited by monsters of our own imagining. Why do we feel so compelled to step out of ourselves and into the frightening attire of someone else? Is it to ward off evil…or to attract it? For children, it is a little of both. Or maybe they just want to feel what it is like to walk in the shoes of a werewolf. Free from parental control, they romp through the night, finding fear exhilarating and vandalism fun!

Is Halloween's true message for mankind lost forever or just temporarily misplaced? Either way, it's important enough to be resurrected. There was a time when October 31st was thought to be the most important night of the year, filled with frightening and yet gratifying manifestations made possible by the rituals of Halloween.

I am descended from a long line of witches dating back to the 1600s, and who better to unravel this tangled web than a witch? My ancestors were "good" witches, and as such I feel an ancient urge within me to set the record straight. Join me. Venture back in time for a moment, and you will see October 31st was once a night of great opportunity that enabled us to view two worlds and choose between them. Is your desire a life of good or evil? Will you choose love or vengeance? This is a "night of change." It is on Halloween that life moves in many different directions.

How far back must we go to find the beginnings of this special holiday? We must look to pagan times, centuries beyond our imagining, dating back to the Druid feasts and festivals. Halloween began as a diversified holiday lasting for days and celebrating more evil than good, but when the Druids were conquered by the Romans, All Hallows Eve remained unaffected.

The Romans must have liked the Druid's festivals as they continued on without interruption. It was after all, the beginning of a new year, a religious holiday when one could atone for wrongdoings of the past year. Or if you were of the opposite persuasion, you could spend the night casting evil spells on friends or family. Times were sinister and barbaric, but under Roman rule barbarism diminished to some degree when the Romans banned human sacrifice, a ritual the Druids were very fond of celebrating.

Unfortunately, sacrificing continued in different ways for different reasons. Animals were put to death to appease the devil or the gods. Black cats, who were thought to befriend witches or even become witches, were put in wooden cages and tossed into blazing fires. That same fate was bestowed on thieves and murderers who were also considered to be no better than animals. This continued well into the Christian era.

The Celtic tribes followed Druid practices throughout England, Ireland, and Wales. During the Roman occupation of Britain, superstition joined forces with the supernatural. This magic mix made October 31st a spiritually dependent holiday. This was an era of reinventing death.

Halloween had a miraculous message that was based on relieving, if not eliminating the ever-present fear of dying. Life was not only short but also difficult. Death was woven into the fabric of everyday living, but few realized it performed a noble service. Death pushed people into living each day to the fullest, ever mindful that tomorrow might not come.

Reincarnation was, to a degree, an accepted belief in medieval times. Many people liked the idea that they had a chance to come back. A return to life on Earth was an interesting concept. However, it was of little comfort to those who were faced with the devastating loss of a child or a loved one. There was no way to instantly activate reincarnation. If only there had been!

However, there were those times when death was viewed in a very different light. Death was not considered a tragedy when it brought to an end a grave illness or horrible accident; it was considered a blessing. If people could not be repaired nor disease cured, death was often a relief. No one wanted others to endure the suffering they knew they couldn't bear themselves.

As Halloween continued to confirm its earthly connections to the afterlife, many still remained skeptical or even frightened of an unknown realm where the ghosts they formerly feared suddenly became unlikely loved ones on October 31st. It took courage to become part of what you couldn't see.

This circle of life became the basis for their ongoing connection to those who had passed on. Each year on October 31st, the dearly departed were welcomed back to Earth to mingle among the living. This was something the living had to look forward to, to plan for, to *live* for. It was a night thick with psychic electricity. Whether seen or simply imagined, the supernatural was willingly accepted. When believable magic filled the air, the moon grew brighter as an invisible curtain rose, and a weight was lifted from life. No longer were the living separated from the dead. The moment had arrived in which to feel the presence of another world.

Among the dark shadows and foggy mist, the living searched the night. Some claimed to have had a fleeting glimpse or vision of a loved one. Others were touched by the gift of a telepathic message. But it didn't matter one way or the other, because in some mysterious way the spirits felt their every thought and heard their every word. "Answers will come. All will be revealed," the wise witches would say.

This is my heritage: witches and witchcraft. It does not come from history books but from stories passed through generations of a family of mystics who have made magic since the beginning of time. There have always been those who've had the gift of miraculous accomplishments: psychics, mediums, mystics, and witches. Whatever you choose to call them, it is comforting to know almost nothing is impossible. Magic is just as available now as it was then.

A NEED TO KNOW

The night is cold
The fog is thick
Is that a noise?
My ears play tricks
We wait, we pray
We search without a clue.
Hoping that they want us to.
In my heart I have no fear.
All Hallows Eve they'll reappear.
Each year commuting to and from.
Is it life or is it death?
That they call home.
I'm not wise.
I need to know.
Which life is best
This or the next?

—Diana Millay

2

Witches and Miracles

Where have all our witches gone? They're still in our midst, making magic every day of the year that once upon a time was thought to happen only on Halloween. But actually, witches practiced their powers every day of the year. Perhaps it was a little more obvious on Halloween.

Magic is as prevalent today as it was in yesteryear, but it often goes unnoticed and almost always unbelieved. Today, people feel they must be able to see what they are asked to believe. And yet, some of life's most extraordinary and mysterious experiences remain forever unexplained...and forever dismissed by non-believers who don't realize that we all make a little magic without even knowing it. By ridding ourselves of the negativity within, we move closer to the supernatural powers that lie dormant in all of us.

Magic is an anonymous attribute that we have a duty to uncover. It's a feeling that arrives when least expected, an urgent need to accomplish. You rise to the occasion or you don't. When something unusual...perhaps magical...happens, have you ever said to yourself, "I can't take credit for that, I didn't do it."? Think again. Maybe you did. Maybe you're a non-believer who has made magic without realizing it!

Perhaps you once grabbed a small child about to slip in front of a moving vehicle. Maybe you saved a life or answered a question that put someone's life on a different path. Witches listen to soul messages, as everyone should. Instinct can produce magic. Don't take the time to dissect it—act on it.

Miracles, big or small, don't take tremendous strength or talent. They take a tremendous desire. I'm not talking about gifts from God; I'm talking about a simple visual endeavor. Small miracles can be accomplished through detailed visualization of exactly what it is you wish to materialize. It takes time and practice. Success is based upon the depth of belief that you have in yourself.

Centuries ago, miracles were part of everyday life. Witches were in demand because they were a necessity. When all else failed, they were the miracle workers.

Giving up was not an option for rural folk who would drive their horse and buggies for miles to visit those they believed had the ability to do for them what thus far had been impossible. There were some who actually uprooted their families to move closer to the "help" they believed they would eventually need.

Witches were amazingly successful because they recognized their powers. Each witch knew what she or he did best. That is not to say they weren't diversified. They were, but in a pinch, any witch would do. However, miracles were greatly increased if those in need of help knew ahead of time which witch did what.

Witches couldn't change the world, but by changing sickness to health, they changed grief to relief. Rarely did witches overstep their boundaries in search of new or different magic, but there were those who specialized: the healers, exorcists, mediums who communed with the dead, those who "talked out fire," and those who predicted the future. They used the powers they were born with because doing so required little or no effort to perform.

Since the beginning of time, good has never been far from evil's reach. Those blessed with miraculous gifts have always been maligned by the skeptics. While many people counted on witches to make miracles, witches were also blamed for anything that was thought to be a misfortune. Often they were labeled "servants of the devil" by those not only filled with jealousy, but also an all-consuming fear of the unexplained. Witches were tortured, hanged, and burned at the stake, while their executioners, professing to be holy, walked free.

Even today, there are those who believe psychics, witches, and healers are con artists. Then again, others believe, all of them, at times to be our greatest saviors. Whatever you believe, good witches have always been ordinary people like the rest of us. Not perfect. Not strange. Not spooky. They marry, raise children, have jobs, plow the fields and tend the animals. Whether their powers were great or small, they used them to the best of their ability and got on with life. They knew what they had, and they knew how to give it away.

3

Rituals of Fire

In ancient times, bonfires on Halloween were of special importance. This was a sacred night, when relatives of the dearly departed gathered around the fires, feasting and dancing in outlandish garb worn to frighten off evil spirits. Black cats and other animals were always sacrificed to the gods on this spiritual occasion—along with humans, who were burned at the stake.

Fire was thought to banish evil spirits and ghosts, all of whom people believed existed although probably invisible to them.

These were primitive times, and All Hallows Eve was a night of both fear and frolic; people were caught between two emotions: their need for fire to survive and second their realization that fire could be responsible, in one way or the other, for their demise. Everyone had duty to the Sun God to keep those fires burning. They never doubted that fire empowered the Sun and kept it shining. They did their part, but there was always a worry that the Sun would not rise.

October 31st was a very busy day in ancient times. Another year meant another chance to mingle with the dead. Food had to be prepared for evening festivities, after which all the home fires were extinguished. At dusk, the ground was cleared, new and sacred bonfires were set ablaze. Torches, padded with peat moss, were lit and passed from house to house. Heat and light were once again restored, never to be put out until next year when Halloween would once again repeat itself. Of course, if such an occurrence did happen and a fire died out, never was it blamed on wind, rain, or storm of night. People believed it was the workings of a witch, of course. Blame was very popular because taking responsibility for even a simple indiscretion was not a good idea. Whether innocent or guilty, male or female, once someone was accused, the result could be disastrous. Fire was uppermost in the minds of everyone…and so was fear. To accuse another of witchcraft was well worth it, to save one's self from being burned alive.

The Sun rose and set by the light of the fires, and that was mankind's first priority. People strongly believed that if the fires died, the Sun would fade into oblivion, and that would be the end of human existence.

Halloween's rituals had a comforting effect because there was no pressure to take part in them or even to believe in their midnight magic. However, people needed to celebrate life and honor the living and the dead. They also had to honor the seasons, which they feared might whither and die if not appreciated. People strongly believed that rituals, intended to control their environment, worked. Where religion let them down, rituals lifted them up. Rituals could be mesmerizing. They were filled with symbolism that was available for the taking. Halloween brought about an annual repetition of what could always be counted on.

At a time when unfulfilled desires were clouded by fear and frustration, Halloween's rituals were there to ignite an important part of existence when most needed. In dangerous and frightening times, rituals struggled to preserve life and extend it by instilling moments of faith when not seeing…is still believing.

On hills, unobstructed by overgrowth, the sacred Halloween bonfires burned. Each was encircled by a freshly dug, shallow trench that was believed to be the size of the Sun. The fire-builders must have been right, because the fires burned contently within their boundaries. Then in the wee hours of morning, the Sun, this indispensable generator of light and heat, would hopefully rise and not only see itself, but also feel the warmth of its own reflection.

The fires were a gift, not only to the Sun but also to humanity. Whether great or small, these fires symbolized the boundaries in life that were not only of benefit to the Sun, but to the living. Halloween remains forever attached to these somehow invasive rituals that were able to make dents in human awareness by opening the mind and activating understanding. Halloween remains forever attached to its rituals.

4

The Power of the Past

My ancestors came to these shores from Holland in 1601, and for them, fire had great significance. My great-grandfather was born with abilities that labeled him a mystic, psychic, witch…but whatever he was called, he was revered by all because he had a special gift: He "talked out fire," My grandmother, who died a short time ago at 102, often spoke of her father's strange abilities. From an early age, she realized he was different.

She never forgot the day when she put her hand on the coal stove not knowing it was hot. Screaming, she ran to her father. Taking her hand in his, he softly mumbled words she couldn't understand as the palm of her tiny hand began instantly to heal over. This was nothing new. Many generations before him had this gift.

When he was a baby, his mother rocked him to sleep in her arms, and she never left her chair to lower the kerosene lamps. She just raised her hand in the direction of the flame. Slowly she lowered it, mumbling a few inaudible words. This was her way of putting out the lights.

His mother—my great-great-grandmother—was also very good at moving objects without moving much herself. If a door blew open, she would raise her hand to push it shut without going anywhere near it. She would summon her sewing from its resting place to wherever it was needed. In the same manner, her footstool made its way to her feet unassisted. Even a sleeping dog might find itself suddenly in the lap of its mistress. All of this and more, was taken for granted. To them, it was a normal part of life.

When my great-grandfather was a drummer boy in the Civil War, fires were rampant and many were out of control. He would approach a fire, mumbling, and by the time he reached it, only the smoldering embers remained. He had "talked it out." This is also exactly what he did when he came upon a buckboard or a covered wagon that was on fire. Often, he not only saved lives, but relieved pain and healed burns in moments.

He was a gentle, soft-spoken man, loved by most, but feared by a few who believed "what he could put out, he could also start." No one in the family thought that was possible because they never saw him do it. In those days, families were constantly lighting candles, stoves, lamps, fireplaces, etc. They would have known if he had the "reverse" ability. Or would they?

This was a family of witches. His grandmother was quite able to start fires as well as put them out. In fact, people in need came from distant villages seeking help from the "witch woman." She predicted the weather, healed the sick, and found the missing. But most intriguing was her ability to cast spells on those who were obese, and those who were addicted to alcohol. The fat lost weight because from then on, their favorite foods made them feel sick, and the heavy drinkers, believe it or not, no longer had a taste for liquor.

The question was always, how long would the spell last? Answers come from dozens of old family letters and diaries as well as the stories that have been passed on verbally, but, until now, never written.

Spells cast were recast if they wore off. Every person was different. In today's world when a prescription runs out, we renew it. This, of course, is costly. In those days, healers wouldn't take money. At least the witches in my family did not. People gave them presents: a chicken, a chair, a pie, their time, or their services. A cow or a horse might be given for saving a life. But nothing was expected and most of the time, nothing was received.

How did they make these things happen? Were they psychic? Of course, but what was most important was that the magic they made was visible, and it was witnessed by others. This gave them credibility, as word spread across the countryside. There were skeptics of course, until one of them needed a witch.

Here is an ancient tale passed on by witches—never written, only spoken:

Missing Parts

Man was born with two ears, two eyes, two hands, two feet, but only one mind and one heart, which was a problem that had to be solved. The second mind and second heart must somehow have been misplaced. Giving this much thought, witches realized that if one had a wife or husband, it was most likely that was where the second heart could, surely, be found, should man ever need it. The second mind was another matter. A Druid wizard had to be consulted. Now the wizard said the second mind could only be found in the next life. How then, man asked, can it be retrieved? It cannot be retrieved, said the wizard. You left it there so you would be able to converse with your ancestors. Have you also lost your memory? Humans are empty vessels through which wisdom flows, said the wizard. Remember to converse with your second mind. It is a much wiser mind than the one you carry around with you. Do this. In the future, you just might become a witch yourself!

5

Saints and Pagans

Within the heart of Halloween lies All Soul's Day and All Saints Day. Shouldn't All Witch's Day be there also? Never mind the fact that both good and bad reside in all of us, including saints and witches. If Halloween's mission is to celebrate the unending existence of our souls and our saints, why not also our witches?

There was a time, long past, when saints and witches were thought to reflect each other in certain ways. While there were males and females of both these persuasions, it was between the women that similarities were most often believed to exist.

Was there really a connection between the over-zealous holiness of cloistered nuns and the unexplained power of witches? Yes, both witches and would-be-saints were able to perform supernatural feats. But not for the same reasons. Also, they both levitated. The nuns did so in an altered state of consciousness. Witches, presumably, rose above ground on broomstick take-offs. However, no evidence exists that witches ever used brooms for anything but sweeping...certainly not for levitating.

Those nuns who chose to actively seek sainthood took a path of personal suffering to get there. They refused food with the exception of bread and water. Extreme fasting not only paralyzes the brain and brings on visions of the worst kind, but also causes a breakdown of the immune system, which is an invitation for disease or possibly an early demise. On the other hand, witches were the opposite. They ate, baked, boiled, and fried. But whether they ate or not, food had nothing to do with their visions.

For the nuns, would it not be more logical to assume that semi-starvation, combined with their belief that self-mutilation made them more Christ-like, probably triggered hallucinations rather than prophetic visions? Nuns believed that from suffering in life they would achieve sainthood in death, and indeed, for some it worked; they became saints. Witches on the other hand had little time to worry about the next life when the present one was barely manageable. They

14

would have been miserable striving for personal perfection in the hereafter. They were present-day achievers. They were channelers, deliverers of change. Their job was to alleviate suffering, not to create it.

However, not many in those days reflected such a clear determination to achieve their goals as did both nuns and witches. Both were held accountable for their actions and both were judged by the end results of those actions. These ladies had guts, at a time when success was not an option for women who were seldom seen and rarely heard.

Is deliberate suffering self-serving or God-serving? Priests were known to be inspired by the nuns' suffering—or perhaps they were unspeakably grateful that they didn't have the same calling themselves. However, when the clergy felt the nuns went too far, the witch/saint connection came through loud and clear. Could it be that while each walked a different path, these women were victims of witchcraft? Or were they creators of it? Where is the divider between right and wrong to be found? Within ourselves? God gives life. Satan gives orders. However, there can be no doubt that suffering, whether self-induced or not, is an all-consuming distraction from life. Leaving unknown greatness…unrecognized.

<u>CHANGING PLACES</u>

EVIL it lives deep down inside
Invented by man
I tried it for size
It fit like a glove
I used it to lie, to rape and to kill
But decades thereafter my toy went downhill
Oh, evil where are you?
We had so much fun
Goodness and mercy are still on the run
I bought a computer, it's karmic I think
It floats in a tub, I hope I won't sink
I logged on to past lives
Lo and behold, I found all my wives
Witches they were, all scrawny and thin
I starved them to death
Before turning them in
Dear karmic computer
Ooh, say you can't see
That my life's almost over
This never could be
So many lifetimes of villainous hate
For more of the same, am I really to late?
Satan and I have always been close
Where is he now?
When I need him most
Hell's here on earth
Heaven can wait
A decade or so?
I promise I'll go
But the answer was no
Shaking I stood

For I knew that I would
Be sentenced forever
To nothing but GOOD.

—*Diana Millay*

6

Hauntings

Death comes to us in many ways: Some are taken suddenly; others succumb to a lingering illness. But when our earthly skin is shed, the soul moves on. Or does it? Not always. Sadly there are those souls who, having left their bodies, have not as yet realized they are dead. Failing to move on, they continue an earthly existence, aimlessly wandering while causing untold damage to people and property. These are "poltergeists," angry ghosts who are still with us. They are spirits who are unable to move on, either refusing to accept death or not realizing that they have died. What greater pain than a life unfinished? Caught between two worlds and unable to control their mindless temper tantrums in death, their presence becomes known to us by their violent ghostly actions.

As a small child, I had a firsthand experience with a very angry ghost. It was on one of many occasions that my mother took me to the "bread lady's" house. On entering her driveway, the smell of baking bread was unmistakable. It was a rambling old house with a huge kitchen lined with cast iron radiators on top of which loaves of bread were rising.

To this day, I can still taste the cookie she gave me as she packed our order. Quite suddenly, from nowhere, a kitchen knife flew across the room all on its own, landing in a wooden cutting board and still quivering as we dashed for cover. Screaming, my mother and I crouched in a corner. The bread lady seemed unfazed as a sack of flower narrowly missed her head. "It's really nothing," she said, as a chair slid across the stone floor. My heart was pounding as I clutched my mother. A large glass cabinet, full of china, crashed to the floor. I held my breath. At last, all was quiet.

An invisible perpetrator had wrecked havoc for what seemed like forever but was probably only a minute or two. The bread lady apologized profusely. "It was only Harold," she said. "The family ghost is usually not this violent. He was stabbed to death by his wife about 100 years ago, and he just never seemed to get over it."

From then on, the bread lady delivered to our home. Shortly thereafter, it was rumored she had hired exorcists to help Harold go to his great reward, but Harold could not be evicted. However, the bread lady was. Her house burned down. The cause was an electrical fire, so they said, but I knew it was Harold.

Don't be misled by my story. Poltergeists can be very dangerous. Either Harold had bad aim or he only intended to frighten us. If you live in a haunted house it is good to remember that the ghosts are the same people they were in life. Their bodies may be missing, but that's all! The soul never dies. Therefore, neither does intelligence, determination, desire, love, hate, good, or evil. Whatever exists in the soul, remains in the ethereal body. Dead or alive, man sees himself exactly as he saw himself in life.

For those who don't know they have died, it can be a traumatizing experience as they spend decades of searching for "home" without a road map. Forever confused, they continue haunting for long-forgotten reasons. However, these tormented souls always have a choice of moving on, or they can remain on Earth and be miserable. Surely to remain must be what is meant by the phrase "Hell on Earth."

Ghosts need not be angry to be active. Often they content themselves with walking through walls, slamming doors, opening drawers, or scaring people. And they do all this for no special reason except, possibly, to make their presence known.

It is in old homes, abandoned or inhabited, such as castles, prisons, monasteries, mansions, or old pubs where ghosts are in abundance. Their haunting hours are generally between midnight and 3 a.m., when they become extremely possessive of their domain—especially if they feel humans are seeking to invade it.

Ghosts haunt places where they have lived or have had a profound experience. Returning to the scene of a crime or simply to a place they left behind, is most common. England and Ireland are probably the most haunted countries in the world. The reason is that to demolish just about any structure older than yourself is not only against the law in these countries, but contrary to the will of the living...and the dead.

Halloween defines death as nothing more than an interruption in life. We simply change location, and we do it three times. When we die, we change location. At birth, we change location, and once again on Halloween, death changes location for a brief time to commune with the living. This makes October 31st the most reliable and predictable holiday of the year. These changes...never change.

My first encounter with a ghost I would describe as somewhat of a see-through apparition. It happened in New Hampshire when I was 15 or 16. I was in a house that was very old, dating back to the Revolution. I had the attic all to myself. No one else was willing to climb all those stairs. The cool New England nights made sleeping a pleasure—with the exception of one night when I woke with a start and felt a draft. I looked to see if my door had blown open. That's when I saw him. He was quite clearly defined, and yet he didn't move, nor did I. This had to be a figment of my imagination.

From my window, the moon cast an eerie glow across the floor. It was at that moment that I knew he wasn't real because he had no feet. He was standing on his ankles. "Please leave," I said, pulling the covers over my head, certain it was a dream.

At breakfast, I couldn't help myself, I burst forth with every detail of my nightmare—only to learn my hosts had forgotten to tell me I wasn't exactly alone in the attic. I had a "companion" who had lived up there for generations. Stunned, I asked, "How did he lose his feet?" When the laughter subsided, they explained that 50 or more years ago the floor was raised when a new roof was put on the house. He still walks on the original floor, they said, which is 8 inches below the new floor. For the duration of my stay, he continued to watch over me. I thought of him as my protector. I learned that whether seen or not seen, these gentle spirits are all around us. Fear not!

7

Witchcraft

Witchcraft requires mental dexterity. A powerful bending of the mind takes place. As the branch bends with the wind, it realigns itself. A witch's mind does the same: It sees the problem, the mind bends, and a correction is made. Sometimes this happens instantly, sometimes it takes longer.

Successfully accomplishing what otherwise would be impossible, is called witchcraft. It is also called sorcery, but there are two sides to everything, and witchcraft is no exception. Sorcery is the dark side. The ability to make things happen has always been serious business, no matter which side you're on.

Witches were hunted down, but could they be eliminated? This was hardly an easy task. The largest part of the population were peasants, and they not only depended on these women, but they trusted them. Witches had much to fear. Their lives and the lives of those around them were literally "at stake." Despite the fact that there were laws against the practice of witchcraft, dating back to the 7th century, witchcraft persisted.

If a farmer's crop froze or his cow disappeared, in the mind of the disgruntled farmer, it could only be sorcery. A witch was to blame. Man and witch had a love/hate relationship. Those who feared the unexplained felt compelled to denounce those whose gifts they secretly desired for themselves.

The great ease with which their magic was made gave rise to jealousy as well as hatred. Even great beauty or unusual talent often sent innocent young girls to the gallows, because it was believed that the devil only distributed such obvious attributes to those who agreed to do his bidding.

In a time when civilization was dominated by males, witchcraft wasn't. In fact, rarely do we hear about male witches, but they existed and yes, they too, were put to death. Horrendous as it was, it seems somewhat surprising that men inflicted the same horrors on their own gender as they did on women.

No one was immune. A witch's success or the lack thereof, were both great excuses to give the devil his due. If the witch was not in league with the devil, there was often a relative who practiced witchcraft or a neighbor who was thought to be a witch. They all would be sentenced to the same fate—death by association.

In the hearts and minds of these women, their "craft" was a gift from God. Given to powerless, but not brainless, females who found a divine mission within themselves by discovering their ability to connect with their subconscious. It was an awakening for some, but not for all.

The supernatural is a phenomenon existing in all of us. It is the one ingredient that witchcraft can't do without, because it is available magic. Directly from the minds eye, a witch sees the visible result surrounding the problem. In the witch's mind, the problem dissolves—something like a mental meltdown, leaving the desired result ready to be transferred to its recipient.

Not every witch made instant magic. It was a craft that was passed on for generations and like other crafts, it required practice. The biggest problem was believing in yourself…knowing that your forefather's genes were your genes, and that they were ready and waiting to be used. Witchcraft came alive while perfecting an in-born creative ability to perform extraordinary tasks. Hopefully, for some, their knowledge of the supernatural kicked in whenever necessary.

Let us not confuse witchcraft with "crafty" witches. A witch referred to as crafty might be described as a sorceress, a cunning, deceitful person leaning toward a darker side of life. Since Satan always had to be appeased, who better to assume that role than a "crafty, self-serving" witch who thought it was in her best interest to secretly cause evil deeds to occur? She would then take credit shortly thereafter, for setting things right. Of course, these crafty witches were always willing to accept a reward as insurance that it would never happen again.

Witchcraft evolved in different ways for different witches. Psychics, often called witches, needed no training or practice. They began talking to voices from the other side of life by the age of 4 or 5. They were also quite able to see the people they conversed with, just as psychics do today.

Although no longer called witches, psychics are still considered a necessity in the lives of many people just as witches were in yesteryear. A large percentage of today's population uses their services on a regular basis. Since the beginning of human existence, they've given their lives to serve others. Many were the victims, in witch-burning times, of unspeakable torture and death, but their souls keep returning to us, because we need them. Today, they are not just tolerated, they are treasured.

8

Witch Doctors

Witchcraft's most important contribution to mankind may have been its witch "doctors." Whether psychic, holistic, or both, these healers devised "recipes" from nature that saved lives then as they do now. The herbs they discovered are very much a part of our medicine today. What we now find in drugstores, witches found in fields of clover and crabgrass. From the poisonous to the edible, they mixed and matched ingredients to make medicine.

Witches discovered purple foxglove for heart ailments. Today it is called Digitalis. Many poisonous herbs, in small doses were the only thing strong enough to fight serious infection. These herbs had the same ability to cure or kill as they do today if you don't follow directions. Ephedra, common today for asthma or allergies, was discovered and used by witches centuries ago.

From the earliest times, witches were midwives. This may be their most important legacy. It is to these women that modern obstetrics will always be indebted. Witch ways were the basis for our present-day birthing methods. Witches discovered Belladonna along with other drugs that are used today to relieve pain during labor and childbirth. Witches led the way it's done today.

Men got medical degrees as early as the 14th century, but men did not monopolize health care for a several hundred years. Witches did. And all the while they were insidiously encroaching on male superiority. Witches made it very difficult for men to reinforce the inferiority of women. They thought this was one more logical reason for getting rid of witches.

Ultimately, male obstetrics put childbirth back in the dark ages, actually, decreasing the population. Thousands of women and babies died for easily avoidable reasons, but mainly, from lack of knowledge and lack of cleanliness, which caused child bed fever. It was a sad time in more ways than one.

If men had been able to find a way to give birth, women would long ago have been extinct. But that didn't happen. The so-called "weaker sex" got stronger, and women actually had the nerve to invade male territory. Since the beginning of time, it was the women who gave life and saved life. They were healers by nature long before doctors or doctorates ever existed.

By the middle of the 17th century, a creeping awareness of women's success in man's supposedly God-given field of medicine became intolerable. More drastic measures were needed as women became a threat, not only to a man's profession, but to their egos. Witch women were considered abnormal. They used unexplainable powers that were undeniably from the devil. If they couldn't be controlled they somehow had to be eliminated. Who better to put an end to witchcraft forever than the Church? Witch women, possessed by evil, had to be stopped.

Therefore, a law was passed permitting only men to practice medicine. The Church decreed that "witch women" would be hunted until the last witch was caught and destroyed. They would then be forced to confess their allegiance to Satan, and then mercifully, they would be sent to their great reward via the gallows or the stake as opposed to lengthy torture.

The Church believed that by denouncing women in public, they might fade into oblivion knowing their alternative fate. But they didn't. They kept a low profile as their underground medicine struggled to rise from the depths of its existence. All the while, they were hunted like animals and subjected to such hideous torture that they would confess to anything. Death was a welcome relief.

For almost 400 years, the lives of these women had been at risk. At least 5 million witches were put death from the 14th through 17th centuries. Perhaps ten percent were men. No one kept count. The Church elders wrote history as they chose for it to be remembered. For years, religion lagged behind a witch's knowledge of God and the universe, but the Church's first priority was not God, it was politics.

Witches were grounded in nature. The Church was grounded in its need to control the living as well as those who they thought should not live. Church officials saw no need to commune with the masses. Why should they? They were much too busy deciding who lived or died. Condemning was the order of the day. While professing goodness and love, the Church set God aside to condone torture and killing.

Church power was feared. They decreed witches to be the creators of evil, but strangely enough, whether witch or not, people were hanged as close to God as possible, in the churchyard. Ultimately religion missed the boat when failing to reinforce what the parishioners already believed. The faithful lost faith and went elsewhere. Some turned to the occult, others to witchcraft. They would try anything in time of spiritual bankruptcy, better still, there was always Halloween, which could be counted on for consolation. Although, it was a long time between Octobers, Halloween's rituals and celebrations could be resurrected on a moment's notice any time of year. Coming together was always possible. However, seeking comfort as well as strength, should have been the job of the Church.

9

Samhain

It is All Hallows Eve from which Halloween takes its name. It's difficult to imagine that its rituals date back to pagan times, but they never arrived in the United States until the mid 1800s. Following the potato famine in Ireland, came the Irish immigration and with them, "Halloween." The Irish also brought to America another much older tradition called Samhain (pronounced sow-en), a witch's holiday that is also celebrated on October 31st for benefit of nature and Mother Earth.

However, in Celtic times, Samhain was a frightening and sinister holiday with festivals lasting for days. Belief at the time was that the gods, not the dead, made themselves as visible and as evil as possible, tricking man into the wrong side of life and into believing there was no way out. Was this Satan's little joke? Whatever it was, both human and animal sacrifices were made to him, to appease the evils surrounding daily life. People were plagued by disease and disasters of nature. Their crops died from lack of rain or from floods, and children died too soon. All this was caused, they believed, by the evil inherent in "nature," which was obviously the work of the gods who were in competition with man.

The celebration of Samhain endured through those primitive, if not practically impossible, times. Could this go on forever? Hopefully not. If evil had been placed in nature by unholy creatures, there must be a way to release it from nature. It was decided that by communing with nature and becoming part of it, there was a chance it would be cleansed and evil would dissolve. We shall never know how, but they did it. They made Earth magic. Evil lives, but it's now above ground. Samhain rose from its own ashes in a time in which no one would have chosen to live.

Samhain was the witches' holiday that celebrated their partnership with nature long before Halloween. To this day, Samhains are the only true guardians of nature we have, for they are not separate from it, but one with it.

Many of us have yet to realize we are related to more than our family; we are related to each other and all living things. "Talk to nature, a stone, a tree, even a few grains of sand," my ancestors would say, "for they are very much alive. Keep them close." They are like our "familiars," the name also given to domestic animals who see beyond life and convey messages.

In ancient times, familiars were feared because they were considered evil spirits. Legend has it that the devil gave birth to them from his ears. If these animals ran away from home, it was said that they were seeking greater rewards for communicating with humans. This was a great excuse for those who mistreated animals. Fortunately, familiars remain in our midst today. You may have one at home. Love them, talk to them, listen to them. Listening is an important part of Earth magic. Silence has much to say.

Samhain's witches call themselves Wiccans today because evil still clings to the word "witch." For me, "witch" is a badge of honor that was passed on by my ancestors who were more like saints than sinners.

Why was witchcraft so inviting? It exceeds the boundaries of ordinary life. Women especially like being able to depend on powers they know to be greater than themselves. In centuries past, when women needed to be liberated from those harsh and cruel times, they sought some form of spiritual transcendence that the Church couldn't provide, but witchcraft did.

If you have a "gift of knowing," it is easy to become possessed with the desire to share it with others. We've all been possessed by something at onetime or another, but not on as grand a scale as Samhain's witches were. What greater service to mankind, than to be possessed by Mother Nature and worship the ground beneath our feet. This is still the message of thousands of Samhain witches for planet and people. We can't live without each other. The question is, will nature continue to rise above man's indifference to it? Yes, as long as we have Wiccans.

Samhain's celebrations remain in the heart of witch country, Salem, Massachusetts, which many Wiccans call home. To this day, their rituals continue to take place on December 22nd, February 1st, March 21st, May 1st, June 21st, August 1st, September 21st, and its most important day, Samhain on October 31st…all reinforcing their sacred commitment to the environment.

Samhain celebrates the seasonal pattern of reincarnation that repeats itself in nature just as it does in human life. Nature comes alive in spring. In summer, it blossoms, and in autumn it slowly fades. This sequence is followed by death in winter only to rise again in spring. It is not a difficult concept, and yet it is rejected by nonbelievers who are determined to denounce what they don't understand.

This circle of life is something nature can't wait to make happen. It's a transformation. The metamorphosis from a caterpillar to a butterfly is a preview of what awaits all of us when death takes a moment to shed a well-used or worn-out body. Life does not cease for a second. Nothing in nature, nothing in life, dies; conditions and locations change, but a man's soul remains forever.

According to legend, it was Jack the Ripper who said to one his dying victims, "You will never feel more alive, than when you are dead." Insane as Jack was, within his distorted mind, did he in some sick way think he could bring death back to life, to satisfy his insatiable craving to kill? If that was so, how strange it was that he stumbled on a fragment of truth. He killed, but his victims lived on.

Knowledge of death is now above ground, but much of life has yet to take notice. Those still demanding proof that life goes on may not *want* to be convinced. Perhaps they are momentarily stuck between fear and acceptance. If you can't keep a step ahead of fear, you're bound to become one with it. There is no point in arguing over what the blind can't see because eventually they will.

All of this is proven not only in nature, but through telepathic communication with a spirit guide or a psychic, but not until one is ready to accept what they can't see or touch. This is something the "modern mind" has trouble doing. As we evolve, the higher conscience takes over, making way for the truth to filter through. Spiritual evolution happens whether you like it or not, and it leads to a higher awareness and greater achievements in each lifetime. How we use ourselves is our choice. It is up to each individual to chose how to live life. We create our own misery, our own glory and our own punishment. In simple terms, we decide whether to be naughty or nice.

10

Coming Back

Hundreds and hundreds of years ago, it was said that Halloween brought the dead back to life. This gave the deceased their own holiday in which to prove that life was everlasting. What Halloween didn't mention was that coming back to life did not only happen on October 31st. This is something the spirits did on a daily basis—always have done, always will do. Whether these returning souls are spirit guides or nosy relations, they like hanging out on earth. Keep in mind when you next encounter a stroke of luck, it could have been with a little help from your guides. Never ignore a spirit helper.

Life is a journey and there are those who progress faster than others. Learning is a process of planting seeds. The trick is allowing them to grow within you. The truth is lodged in the subconscious. Visual proof of transformation is the butterfly rising from its cocoon. Death is just another part of life at which time we shed the physical body. What a relief! To travel unencumbered is a joy unknown in the physical realm and the very reason why there are those on the other side who sometimes decide not to return to physical life. It's a personal choice. Life is temporary, but so is death.

Amidst the vast unknown, is an afterlife virtually littered with questions. Where do we find the spirit world for earth souls? Is the astral plain so vast that we may never find each other when we get there? Not to worry. The other side of life is governed by telepathic communication. To think or to visualize a person in the afterlife is to see them. It's an instant coming together. It's the ultimate personal connection that's constantly available, and is similar to a soul-review, except that reviewing your soul is a conversation with yourself. It could be the most important or most valuable part of death. A soul-review is a life reviewing itself. Every second of every minute spent on Earth, everything we've done or failed to do from birth to the end of life, passes before our eyes in living color. It is definitely an opportunity to be your own shrink and analyze yourself. The joy created, the pain inflicted, is all on your very own "soul tape." As a bonus, you look back on your past lives as well. We learn so much from soul-reviewing. It's a pity we don't remember some of it in the next life. Or do we?

This is a period of evolution when the soul reflects on desires and ideals retained from earth life. It's heaven if a soul chooses to see it that way—somewhat in the nature of a magnificent dream, but nonetheless real. It's a reunion of souls, where it is said dislike, revenge, rivalry, earthly animosities dissolve on arrival. Rather like growing up, we rise above it all as the ego is laid aside. Can we attribute differing religious thinking as a hindrance in man's endless efforts to find the truth? That's doubtful, but religions do tend to teach only half the truth. It's Halloween that leads us to the other half.

In the afterlife, deities are not center stage, following a leader is non existent because there is no leader, but there are guides and spirit helpers as there are on Earth. Freedom abounds, death continues to leave life up to the individual. It's your choice. Cherished beliefs and old traditions die hard, but the afterlife is a time for mentally discarding what is no longer of use. You have guides as well as friends and relatives that have left the living. You're not alone unless you want to be.

If you believe that death delivers you from responsibility, think again. We are as responsible in death as we were in life. If you were not a responsible person in life, you will be in the afterlife. Death is a busy place, and it's also a place of business where agreements, contacts, and decisions are all very much a part of the hereafter. But unlike life, there are no secretaries to hire. Not only do we "sign" contracts, we write them. Actually, we make deals, which are in fact agreements we make with ourselves.

We make these contracts for our next life and we are expected to fill them. Whether to serve others or ourselves, there are karmic debts to be paid. We have promises to keep. The question arises, how will I remember them? Circumstances will appear at a time and place suitable for success. Will you honor your contract or not? It's up to you. Perhaps this is one reason why we have so many lifetimes. We keep coming back until we get it right.

ASK THEM

Whispering sounds
Souls hovering round
Asked to appear
Suddenly here
Could we be wrong?
Were they here all along?
Please ask them to stay
Don't send them away
Knowing it's they
Who will teach us the lessons
Of yesterday.

—Diana Millay

11

Enlightenment

On October 31st, both Samhain and Halloween have always sought to reconnect people with their ancestral souls in the hereafter and to reclaim the lost knowledge everyone hoped they had to share. We can only guess what these souls might have conveyed. Something comforting, easy to digest, such as "What would life become without death?" Without death, there would be no lessons, no discoveries, no advancement, and no way to realize who we are or who we wish to be.

This leads us to believe that astral living is a continuing personal advancement. A period of development and exploration as well as a search to understand that which lies dormant in the soul. At death, the soul awakens to this new experience. Enlightenment begins when belief and understanding is ready to be retained.

Long ago, Tibetan Buddhists reminded mankind of two things in life that were important at the time of death. First, while in the physical world, we must take time to consider that what we've done in our life is not as important as the effect that it has had on others. This is karma. What goes around, comes around. Is karma unavoidable? The good news, according to these Buddhists of old, is that that when death is imminent, karma is not entirely beyond remedy. If a soul is truly repentant and not just scared "to death" of hell, fire, and brimstone, karma may be reduced…to a degree. In other words, a change of heart before moving on is a necessity. I'm only guessing, but these Buddhists may have meant, the sooner the better, depending on the amount of karmic debt one has to pay.

Don't die in a rage or in fear. Die peacefully. Don't panic. Leaving life is equally as important as coming into it, but not nearly as stressful. Once again, the cord is cut. There are no ties when you enter or exit life; you are on your own. We bring no baggage and take none when we leave. A smooth transition comes with an uncluttered mind. We don't forget, but we do mentally detach from possessions, from friends and loved ones left in life. Death should be approached as a journey. It's a relief. Life carries a heavy load; death doesn't.

Wasn't it the Dalai Lama who said, "Never worry about becoming non-existent. Worry about your final thoughts as you slip away. They have ability to affect a positive or negative beginning in the hereafter." I don't wish to dwell on the ins and outs of death, except to say that as we are drifting out of here, we are never alone. When making this transition, every soul is accompanied by a spirit guide, or a loved one who has passed on.

When Halloween was young, and skepticism was not man's first thought, life wasn't willing to detach itself from the dead. Reincarnation held the two together. While separate from religion now, it wasn't separate then. Reincarnation has remained alive in the world to this day. In the United States, about 65 percent of the population believe in reincarnation.

12

Halloween's Magician

In the late 1800s, those living in the Victorian Era were obsessed with the occult. Spirituality and contact with the spirit world in particular were things many people wanted to be part of. Séances were as popular as movies are today. They were available in haunted houses complete with ghosts of your desire. Was it fact or fiction? A majority of séances were trickery, but real or imagined, if the tricks were believed, the purpose was served. If people got what they wanted, trickery became truth. Perhaps this was Halloween's introduction to commercialism—without losing its spiritual message or its life, it slipped into the 20th century.

In a decade or two, life changed drastically. Women emerged from the kitchen and made something of themselves. They were thwarted at every turn but stood their ground. Fortunately, they no longer had to worry about being "burned at the stake."

The time had finally come when séances and phony mediums were exposed by none other than the world's most famous magician, Harry Houdini (1874-1926).

Houdini was a spiritualist and possibility a psychic who took on the job of exposing fraudulent mediums. He succeeded by putting their names in print which put them out of business. Some left town before the sheriff caught them, but many went to jail. The séance fad had diminished when the first World War came and women not only went to work, but they picketed until they got the right to vote. It was the Roaring Twenties…women spread their wings and shortened their skirts.

Alas, in 1926, a happy country was saddened by a dying Houdini, who was suffering horribly from an undiagnosed ruptured appendix. Before finally slipping away, he made a promise to his wife that he would find his way back to her. He even gave her a secret code and a designated time and place. His wife, and the world, waited patiently, actually for years, but without any sign of Harry. Personally I think he came back, but being new at materializing, he didn't realize the amount of ectoplasm he needed to manufacture in order to become even a shadow of himself. Haunting takes practice. Tapping out codes might even have been more difficult for him.

To the very end, the great Houdini made magic, even taking care to exit life on the appropriate holiday. He died on Halloween. The country mourned. The world let sleeping spirits lie. Death refused to take a holiday, but for a brief moment, October 31st, 1926, became Houdini's Halloween. No doubt, he will always be a part of its magic.

13

Halloween History

As Halloween's most distant origins are Druid, Samhain's routes in Ireland with the Celts may be even earlier. The Celts were nomadic tribes who spread themselves over Europe and the British Isles. They were constantly on the move and always ready for a fight. They were fierce and formidable. In fact, there was no getting rid of them. They were true warriors who fought for their lives throughout the world. They made their mark and left it for eternity. It might be hard to find a country today without a Celtic connection.

Celts celebrated with the Samhains on October 31st when the barn doors were opened and the cows came home. It was about to become winter. Fires were lit not only to ward off evil spirits, but to warm the hearts and hands of man. The feast of Samhain was not fun and frolic, but a sinister holiday. The women cooked and tried to make merry as human and animal sacrifices were tossed in the fire. It was diversified madness that also incorporated the Christian feast of All Hallows Eve. Add paganism to the pot, stir, and see the future of Halloween well equipped with good and evil, both necessary ingredients for Halloween's survival.

While stirring the pot, let us not forget another ingredient that quite possibly could be the mother of all Halloweens. In medieval times, Samhain may have been responsible for its birth. Without warning, Samhain insidiously turned reincarnation inside out. It raised the dead. The Druids were the first to take a keen interest, but Halloween celebrants picked up the ball and have never stopped running with it.

In dark and distant times, everyone celebrated together. The living along with the spirits roamed the countryside visiting friends and families. Although they were only vaguely visible to the living, together they made much more than mischief. Spirits or not, these elusive creatures were actually held responsible for their actions. How is this possible? How could spirits be as destructive as people? Whether they were or not, it suggests that these spirits might have been "human pretenders" appearing to be ghostly spirits. Costumes and pranks had not been recently invented. There is no reason to believe they were not as much a part of Halloween then as they are now.

The Druids might very well have been game for all of this, as they were more open-minded at a time when few were. Druids were spiritual folk. Although not attached to a particular belief, they were a powerful and influential clan who freely expressed their views.

Believe it or not, Druids favored equality among genders, but to what extent we may never know. We can only assume that like the Celts and the Samhains, it took awhile before they managed to separate the sinister from the sacred. Time passed before the primitive mind realized that the sacrificial killing of humans and animals brought no rewards to the living, to the dead, or to Halloween.

At some point, this Brotherhood of Druids must have done something right because their descendents are found today not just in Britain but throughout the world. Well-equipped with wisdom, Druids claim to have originated on the island of Atlantis. After its destruction or demise, the Druids suddenly rose up and re-entered life in Egypt and Britain.

Between the 1st and 2nd century, the British Order of Druids came into being and flourished. It is said that these Druids founded more than 25 seats of learning throughout Britain, which today are thriving communities. It seems obvious the Druids were not only incredibly good teachers but incredibly gifted mystics. They turned Wizardry into Druidry, which was a philosophy they combined with psychic science. This was not a religion, although a majority of Druids were priests or ministers. Could it have been the early beginnings of the separation of Church and state? If so, it was definitely not the separation of state and spirituality. In fact, the Druids believed achievements in life would be judged in the hereafter to the extent man had spiritually evolved and thereby, the advancement of civilization.

For centuries, Druids went through good and bad times. They were seriously persecuted in the times of Augustine (around 600 A.D.), almost to the point of extinction. Under their Roman conquerors, they also barely survived. It was a long road of many lifetimes before the people realized these primitive mystics were ahead of their time. They survived by their wits, and their innate ability to always see a light at the end of the tunnel. The Druid mind had no boundaries, which helped them break through those in life.

In prehistoric times, everyone worshiped something. There were goddesses and gods who oversaw everything in life—a goddess of heaven, goddess of birth and everything in between. The Celts worshipped what they depended on most, the Sun God. There was even a time when Christianity considered God to be both male and female. Women ran monasteries and held other high positions in the Church. Times were changing. The day of the woman was short-lived.

Christianity could not rid the world of paganism, however although in the 5th century Saint Patrick tried his best to convert them, but there were just too many pagans. The Irish wanted to reward Patrick for his efforts. Hard put to think of a way, they commended him for banishing snakes from Ireland. Whether Patrick knew it or not, there were few if any snakes in Ireland. It's a country surrounded by salt water. Even if the snakes had flown in, the poor creatures would have died of thirst looking for fresh water.

However, pagans were still in abundance, and integration became the name of the game. The Church decided that Christian and pagan gods would become one. The two joined forces, as did pagan and Christian holidays. Their dates remained the same, but their names were changed to appease devout Christian followers. December 25th, a pagan holiday, suddenly became Christ's birthday. This was clever public relations. The Church knew how to draw in the multitudes. For pagans, December 25th had always been the Sun God's feast day, and so it remained for the pagan worshipers, who arrived in droves.

As time passed, life reversed itself as Christians began to outnumber pagans. The remaining pagans became Christians because they had no choice. Cohabitation was no longer in fashion. Integrate or eradicate were the only two options. Atrocities in the name of God were excuses the Church used to condone its inhumanity to man. Instead of worshipping God, they used Him for less-than-holy purposes.

14

Salem Witch Trials

Salem, Massachusetts, is a living reminder of its own senseless atrocities when, in 1692, nineteen women were accused of being witches and hanged on Gallows Hill. Although this is very few in comparison to the five million witches burned at the stake, killing the innocent will always cry out for eternal attention. Salem's Memorial is entrenched in commercialism. This is not a bad thing because even their ghoulish souvenirs force us to remember what never should have happened.

In those brutal days of human sacrifices, good and evil lived too close together. The question of which to follow was obvious, but in the 17th century, decisions great or small would quickly be resolved by death. Human life was insignificant. Torture and brutality were in the hands of men who, lacking in wisdom, reveled in power.

We may never know why men were frightened by witches and witchcraft. Granted neither was easy to understand. Was witchcraft a gift or a curse? Men feared that witches gave birth to evil in "girl children," and they had to be put to death. By doing so, men became the very thing they feared most: demons.

I have a strange feeling that victims of the witch trials still mingle among the living in Salem. It is not uncommon for spirits to return to the scene of a crime, particularly in a sudden death or brutal killing if they believed themselves to be innocent. A death too violent to remember falls into the category of unfinished business for the victim. Some souls need to view and dissect their demise. Other souls may be too traumatized to move on…no longer raging or resentful, but still unable to shake off the physical. In other words, a ghost in shock looks for a way to rewrite his own death.

The nineteen victims hanged in Salem were women. The twentieth victim was a male also presumed to be a witch. It is said he was tossed in a ditch and heavy stones were placed over his body until he passed into the next life. Compared to this, hanging would have been a blessing.

This was an era in which people believed the supernatural existed, but they were deathly afraid of it. How could they not be when so little in life could be explained? There was nothing between good and evil. You were one or the other, but it wasn't of your own choosing. Judging and hatred were two favorite pastimes of Salem's town folk. The victims' accusers were only children, nevertheless, they were responsible for inciting insanity in themselves—a "disease" that quickly spread.

It all began in early 1691 when a pastor's young daughter began acting somewhat like an animal, drooling and growling. Her elders sought an explanation for her contortions and inaudible babbling. It could be only one thing; a witch had cast a spell on her. This poor child got so much attention that others wanted in on the act. In rapid succession other children quickly succumbed to this attention-getting disease. Charges were made left and right. Most of the women accused were the least likely to be witches and totally unable to defend themselves. They were either poor, deranged, or disliked. It was an easy excuse to get rid of an annoying neighbor.

All the while the "girl's disease" was on the rise, and they loved every minute of it. Addicted to the spotlight, they invented new afflictions. They claimed to have been bitten, fondled, and pinched in peculiar places, but of course there were no witnesses. These kids weren't dumb. They were cunning and conniving. They claimed the perpetrator was invisible. It happened at night in their own homes where they screamed for their mothers. But the invisible ghost was always gone along with the evidence, bite marks, etc., before mummy and daddy arrived on the scene.

History fails to blame this inappropriate haunting on the one man who was stoned to death at the witch trials. It is doubtful the girls would have accused a woman, but someone had to pay the price even for being invisible—and he was the only male witch put to death. Even after the hangings, the children continued to accuse ghosts, as well as people, of ludicrous acts. Eventually, some town folk began to realize that these children were craving the attention they never got in those days. These kids had taken over the lives and minds of grownups and promptly put into practice their parent's evil ways.

Every year, witches and non-witches take part in a candlelight vigil where the hangings took place on Salem's Gallows Hill. This centuries-old backdrop once again became a cozy meeting place for the living and the dead. This is a strange experience for some. What is seen or not seen, is in the mind's eye.

Salem's legacy may well be worth the longest and largest Halloween celebration in the world. The city is a modern day Mecca for the entire month of October, if not year-round, complete with amusement attractions which include costumed monsters and vampires roaming in and out of haunted houses, and yes, even Dracula's Castle is open for inspection. "Hollywood" has come and gone, as do over a million people every year.

Have a question? Have no fear, a witch is near—at those irresistible Wicca vending booths along with shops selling occult, New Age and Old Age. There's something for everyone. While the city fathers are neither addicted to witchcraft nor apt to become witches, they are no doubt devoted to the immense influx of money generated by Salem's legacy that flows into the city's pocket, temporarily sedating an unending desire to rid themselves of witches.

Salem is diversified. If history is your interest, there is plenty of it. The Salem Witch Museum houses a fascinating chronicle of torture, executions, and trials complete with dramatic narration and sound effects. The tour takes half an hour and not a minute longer because the next group of tourists anxiously awaits. Not to worry, the museum exit is the entrance to a sizeable and fascinating gift shop where you can shop 'til you drop.

The appropriate spooky eateries are also plentiful. Afterwards, to lose those calories, take a walking tour of Salem's grim and haunted past. Stroll through cemeteries and buildings complete with ghostly narrators. If you wish to scare yourself to death, take an evening tour where atrocities actually occurred and where in the dark of night, vampires are guaranteed to roam. This is a place where old souls feel right at home, and that's what we all are.

Don't miss the wax effigies. If you like your ghosts up close and personal, this is the museum for you. Some are so well crafted, I'm sure they come alive at midnight. As a change of pace, the Peabody Essex Museum is a repository of Salem's history. Original documents are on-hand from records of misdemeanors to trials and other atrocities. It would be interesting to know if crimes both great and small received equal punishment. Fortunately this is the place that separates fact from fiction. If it happened in Salem, the proof is at the Peabody.

Prior to Salem's Hollywood makeover, it was a sleepy little town. In the early 1950s when I was a young child, my family and I toured Salem in one day. One eerie moment stands out in my memory. It happened in Nathaniel Hawthorne's "House of Seven Gables," which is still open to the public, but in those days there were no guides, no guards, and very few people. We got tickets and wandered around for as long as we wanted. I loved it. It was like going to my grandfather's house. I felt at home, and being an inquisitive child, I strayed from my parents peering into every nook and cranny and opening every door.

I remember the upstairs smelled musty. I tried opening a window but they must have nailed it shut. I found candy wrappers under chair cushions, and I discovered a dead mouse in a drawer, which I put in my pocket. I had one last closet to investigate. I twisted and pulled on the knob, but it wouldn't open. I pulled harder. The door flew open and I landed flat on my back. As I sat up I thought I saw someone, but the closet was dark and deep. I stared until what I thought I saw vanished. I brushed myself off and closed the closet door just as my parents reached the landing. Pleased with myself for not being a bit scared, I said, "You just missed it. I saw a man through a wall." "Really?" my father said, smiling. "It must have been a ghost!"

Few people these days know that Nathaniel Hawthorne (1804-1864) had close family ties to the witch trials. In fact, they were too close for comfort. He had a relative named John Hathorne who was one of the magistrates who presided over the witch trials. It is said that Nathaniel never got over his close ancestral connection to this tragedy. He not only wrote a novel about it (*The House of Seven Gables*) but he changed the spelling of his name to the way it's spelled today, believing this would cut the ancestral cord, and hoping his readers would never find the sinful connection in his past.

15

Dependency Day

I think modern-day Halloween should be renamed "Dependency Day." Whether we realize it or not, we depend on Halloween to release us from ourselves. To leave our bodies and enter another, we dress up on Halloween. This dramatic change is no longer to please the dead but the living. What could be more exciting than to walk among friends and feel what it's like to be anonymous? Follow the way of the actor to understand what it's like to think with another's mind and live in another's body. You can become anything you want. All it takes is changing your costume and your thinking.

In the early days, people made every effort to be acceptable to the dead. They aimed to please, ever mindful that they might be next to cross over. Today we no longer have to please anyone, not even our parents—only ourselves. We can choose exactly who we want to be. In costumes, we can be outlandish or lavish, animal or vegetable. Children sometimes have trouble deciding who they are, let alone who they want to be.

The idea of stepping out of our "solitary confinement" to become something else is one of Halloween's most cherished and dependable attributes. Camouflaging identity allows kids time to become free spirits—time to investigate how it feels to be an angel, a witch, or just themselves with no strings or parents attached.

To those who say Halloween has lost the power it had in the old days and needs to be redeemed, I say, nonsense! Halloween doesn't need redemption, it provides it! It's a very good thing that Halloween's early religious affiliations have been severed, and it's an even better thing that its spiritual connections remain intact. This is a powerful holiday that has never allowed technology to leave reverence in its wake. Halloween is a glory train for all to jump on.

Life separates people, but the week of October 31st brings people together, especially at malls and markets. Cash registers overflow as early Halloweeners swing into action. Costumes these days are not only for kids but for moms, dads, and even the family dog, so that they can tag along with children and not be recognized as parents.

The Irish barely set foot on U.S. soil before unpacking Halloween's traditions. It was just about all they brought with them. The Irish famine had left them poor and starving, and they arrived in that condition. Perhaps it was their desperation that gave birth to what we know today as "trick or treating." It was not only on Halloween, but many other days that they walked for miles asking for money, food, and clothing, in lieu of tricks.

In those days, it was not yet a children's holiday, but one in remembrance of the dead for whom the women baked "soul cakes." Made of oatmeal and molasses, these cakes didn't taste very good. Nor were they much improved with the later addition of dried fruits. But these little cakes had a twofold purpose. The hungry went from house to house begging for them while those who baked them went house to house selling them. No doubt there were some who begged for them, and then sold them. These little cakes got around. Their final resting place was often the cemetery where they were laid to rest with the dead, for whom the cakes were originally baked.

Our most enduring Halloween traditions are of Irish origin, most of which, at the time, were opposed or strictly forbidden by the Church. Telling fortunes and practicing witchcraft—in fact, magical acts of any kind—were against the law. Ghosts were believed to be found in the minds of the mentally disturbed, who were forced by the church to be isolated "for their own good." The church made every effort to keep October 31st an austere religious holiday for as long as possible.

By the 20th century, the Church had to lighten up or loose its audience. An Irish Halloween had taken hold. Fairy costumes were in as much demand for girls as monster costumes were for boys. The old rituals slipped away as it became a children's night for fun and frolic, tricks and treats. The darker the night, the easier to scare yourself and others.

Freedom without control will always be a huge Halloween treat that children depend on. The ability to walk around unrecognized is a prelude to the possibilities available in life—a frog today, a princess tomorrow. It's a view into the future of a child's own making, always leaving life with things to look forward to.

While the British and Scottish might have liked a little more credit for their involvement in Halloween, the prize goes to the Irish. They not only brought with them, the name Halloween, but they included their own traditions as they went about Americanizing themselves. They not only believed in everything magical, but they depended on fairies, goblins, and their "little people" to reminded us not to grow up, not to grow old, and not to stop laughing.

16

Irish Jack

The Irish had a story for every occasion, and this is a tale to remember:

> Once upon a time, there was a nasty old man called Irish Jack. Now, Jack was in league with the devil, who helped him steal crops and destroy anything in his way. Not only was Jack mean and stingy, he was disloyal even to the devil. No wonder Jack was worried about dying and going to Hell. So he tricked the devil into climbing an apple tree to pick some fruit. While the devil was picking, Jack tied two sticks together with a rag and fastened them to a branch. The sign of the cross was in the devil's face. Jack made the devil swear that he would never attempt to claim Jack's soul for himself. The devil agreed. Jack removed the cross and the devil jumped out of the tree.
>
> When it came time for Jack to go to his great reward, he found himself at the gates of heaven. But lo and behold they were locked. There was nothing for him to do but head back to Hell. However the devil refused to let him in. The devil kept his bargain. "You made me promise," said the devil, "not to claim your soul. Now you are doomed to haunt the living. But I have something for you: a few hot coals from the fires of Hell to keep you warm."
>
> Jack walked all the way back to Earth with the hot coals in his hand still warm and glowing. Back on his own turf, he was up to his old tricks. He stole a large turnip. He scraped out the innards, cut holes in its sides, made a handle of vines, and tossed in those glowing coals from Hell. Finally, Jack had done something good. He had turned a vegetable into a nightlight. He still wanders the earth, but never without his invention, the "Jack-o'-Lantern." With his eternal light, Jack became the world's night watchman.

Time passed before Jack-o'-Lanterns were in every window and on every door-step. Though they were rare in Jack's time, pumpkins to carve were in as much demand as pumpkin pies were to eat. While the dead no longer held the spot-light, the devil's ratings also dropped as kids clamored for devil costumes, which was a great excuse for Halloween mischief. These children without realizing it, diminished the "devil's wrath" by mass-producing him on Halloween. When no two devils ever looked alike, his image began to fade. As his powers were ridiculed, he became somewhat of a joke.

Costumes can have a great impact. Especially when they are copied from life, it's very possible for them to become powerful symbols of the real thing. Necessity is the mother of invention, and in medieval times that is exactly how costumes came alive—by necessity. Poor people and poor churches could not afford statues or even replicas of the saints, which they desperately needed to parade through the streets on All Saints Day. To be empty-handed would have been unthinkable. But to dress like saints might be even more effective, and so it was. Parishioners and Church officials got their message across. The saints came alive through the power and determination of those in costume.

17

Then and Now

In the early 1900s, many of Halloween's early rituals had fallen by the wayside, either because they were too much trouble, too scary, or people were just too busy. At the same time, tricks and treats were on their way to becoming an everlasting ritual, while the ever-popular practice of fortunetelling took a back seat.

This was a time when apples were in abundance and used for many purposes—among them, predicting the future. Apples are sacred to witches and were thought of as magical. The witches in my family would sit around the fire peeling them while mumbling this incantation:

> I peel in circles until I find
> My lover's name
> On smoldering rind
> If not I find
> A name
> That gives me peace of mind
> I'll peel all night
> With a sharpened knife
> For my true love
> I'd give my life.

Apples are versatile little creatures. My ancestors loved to pick them and turn them into "shrunken heads." They are not difficult to make, but shrunken apple heads should be carved three weeks ahead of time, because that's how long they take to shrink. Peel several large apples. Remove enough of the core so that a stick will go straight through the center of the apple. To make the face, don't cut out eyes. Make indentations around each feature so that eyes, nose, and mouth pop out at you as the face shrinks. Make deep wedges around the edges and corners of the mouth. Thin forehead lines are attractive, as are deep furrows above the nose. Make each apple a little different. You can make wedges around ears so that they protrude, and use straw for hair. Put a sturdy stick through the center of each apple. Stand each one up in glass jars or a large bowl and let them dry out. You can decorate them if you want, but I prefer my shrunken heads rustic and unadorned, they may look a little weird but they are magical. Ask the Earth gods, and ye' shall receive.

Acorns have always been regarded as sacred, both then and now according to old and new witches. In the days of witch burnings, the acorn was to witches what an I.D. card is today. If you wanted to let someone know you were a witch, you put an acorn in their hand. Acorns are the powerful offspring of the oak tree, which also provides the gift of protection to those in need. These little "witch fruits," as acorns are sometimes called, strangely enough, also have the power of invisibility—something a witch desperately needed. I can only say that the closer you are to an acorn, the better. They bring life into your home and love into your life. Plants bloom in their presence, and so do people.

This and more springs forth from the mighty oak. If you have an oak tree on your property, treasure it and talk to it. Every New Age person is talking to trees these days, but I guarantee the oak is the only one that talks back. The Druids and the Celts worshipped the oak for its magical powers. It is most likely that modern day Druids still do.

Many nature lovers and Halloween enthusiasts are aware that power exists in a tree that has been struck by lightening. For centuries witches have used the branches to make "magic wands." However, I don't think my ancestors would have known what to do with a magic wand. They were farmers and probably would have used it as a cattle prod. Nevertheless, when lightening strikes, electricity is injected, no matter what kind of tree nature plugs into, its composition is forever changed.

Lightening not only increases its power, but it changes the "feel" of the wood. When the electricity within us connects with the electricity in the wood, I can't guarantee magic, but you may find life has fewer obstacles. Electrified wood makes the ride smoother.

When a storm subsides, don't wait for the rain to stop. Rush outside and pick up those fallen branches. It's even better if branches are pulled down or broken off the tree because when they are left on the ground, the energy is absorbed by the earth. But not quite all of it. Don't throw away any wood that's been struck by lightening. Some of its energy may have dissipated, but a certain amount is likely to remain and bring good luck.

18

Spiritual Consumerism

The grandest display of witches today can be found at home in the heart of witch country—a place where there is absolutely no sign of population burnout, and the physical landscape shows little sign of wear and tear. Even in the hectic month of October, its inhabitants cleverly hide any display of fatigue by contenting themselves with Salem's bottomless pit of abundance. All the while its demonizers are cavorting with the psychics, because if they didn't, like witches, the demonizers would be reduced to ash.

You might say that Salem's massive success is, in some measure, a sacred enterprise due to Samhain's witches. Some 3,000 of them call Salem home—along with Christians and a more recent influx of religious zealots who always arrive with a message they somehow fail to get across, because the gods of free enterprise and commercial success manage to keep Salem healthy, wealthy, and wise.

It was consumerism that gave birth to Salem's commercialism in the 1980s when people just couldn't find enough to buy. They couldn't get their fill of witches and witchcraft. They would have bought the earth beneath their feet had it been for sale, because Salem's soil is symbolic. Feeling, touching, and seeing it activates understanding and confirms the belief that Salem has a lot for people to digest besides its wicked ways.

Consumerism in Salem carries with it a message. It's a human cry for the return of that which is missing in life. It's not the dead. It's more of a spiritual integration that does not interfere with daily life, but is an essential part of it. There are still missing pieces, and Salem is a trough for the thirsty. To some, Salem is an upscale flea market. To others, it's a religious experience, where they can go to commune with what might have been their roots. What better place could one go to dig for a connection to what they feel is missing in their life? They've come to the right place. Salem aims to please, but it's not the "customers" they attract. It's "consumers" who devour everything in sight, in an effort to satisfy a human craving for that which is beyond the boundaries of ordinary life.

Salem is the site of a 365-day Halloween party. It's an open invitation to what exists and what doesn't—quite possibly outdoing the world's most famous Halloween party: Queen Victoria's Halloween Bash in 1874. It took place at Balmoral Castle in Scotland. She planned the event herself, and then ruled over every detail from start to finish in the same determined manor she ruled her kingdom.

The Queen's lavish preparations and attention to detail may have run a close second to her coronation. Masked Balls were nothing new to her. Nor were holidays, which she believed she was born to celebrate.

October of 1874 was a Halloween to remember. The Queen invited not only friends and royal relatives, but also her tenant farmers and castle servants to join her in a torchlight procession around the palace grounds. They walked while she rode in a four-wheel, horse-drawn carriage. With a fiery torch in every hand (including the Queen's), this strange but exotic procession was only the beginning. How cleverly she had set the stage for her indoor celebration: Balmoral by candlelight. It must have been hard to tell the ghosts from the guests.

Queen Victoria always left them wanting more, and that's exactly what Salem does. Every day of the year, Salem, in its own way, surpasses Victoria's one very enchanted evening by supplying the unknown but never explaining it.

Salem not only has Halloween to celebrate, but it has the magic of Samhain which defines the true nature of witches from ancient days to the present. There was a time when witches counted on the Earth to provide them with the herbs needed to make medicine. Now the Earth is counting on all of us, not just witches, to preserve and protect it. Today's witches believe that human life is but a small part of nature's ever-present perfection. Samhain is nature worship, not just for witches, for everyone. It asks nothing, but gives so much that we take for granted. From day one, witches looked after nature first and themselves second.

Whether you're a witch or average person, having powers is one thing, but how you choose to use them is what counts. Why is it then that witches today are still subject to ridicule? The answer is "the birds pick at the best fruit." Success beyond explanation encourages attacks from the skeptics and the jealous who always rush to condemn witches who are never in a rush for anything...except maybe justice.

19

A Changing Image

Glancing back through the pages, I find so much I've left unsaid. But this is not the last chapter, for that's an experience Halloween will never have. This has been a brief pause, a short summation of what Halloween has made possible for the living and the dead.

Time cannot be reversed, but life and death can. Halloween already reversed both of them, at a time when life was caught between fear and desire for one or the other. The aura of Halloween put death smack in the center of life. The living saw the dying leave their bodies and walk away, but they didn't go far. Is it really possible to walk in and out of life? Of course it is, because at death, life reverses itself from matter to spirit in the flicker of an eye, changing the image of death. As time passed, Halloween changed course as its image changed from mourning death to celebrating unending life.

Modern Halloween has a life of its own over which we shall never gain control and never should. Despite the efforts of religious extremists and nervous mothers, Halloween has no rules and sees no use for those made by man. Crime does not equal punishment on Halloween. Small cities have parades or organized celebrations to attract those who like tidy and predictable holidays. This does not fit Halloween's job description. We depend on Halloween to be unpredictable...forever changing its image.

This is the only night of the year that we're allowed to run wild. On second thought, isn't that exactly what we do on the other 364 nights when we're not in costume? Halloween housewives are no longer obligated to spend the day in the kitchen with soul cakes or nights in the cemetery with the dead.

There were those who at one time chose to label Halloween morbid or depressing, in an era when Satanic cults chose Halloween for their midnight sorcery. Incantations around a bonfire sprang not from the rising Sun, but from the fires of Hell. Today, Halloween's image is very well lit by millions who spend billions on their favorite holiday, which is reinvented every year. There is no way can we reuse last year's pumpkins, and while boys may prefer to be vampires year after year, girls wouldn't be caught "dead" in the same costume. Halloween cannot be compared to traditional holidays. Its commercial explosion is a relatively new experience. Strangely enough, it is not popular with religious folk who still see Satan in the midst of Halloween fun. They would prefer to have it celebrated under more sacred supervision.

Halloween is a wonderful melting pot of immigrants who continue to bring their customs along with their pranks and laughter. Halloween was always a night to let off steam, perhaps it still is. It is a night revamped by each generation. In the 20th century its rough edges were smoothed, and it became more respectable. It's difficult to believe there was a time when clever businessmen dreaded holidays because they lost money. Obviously, this was before they learned how to capitalize on the special consumer desires that come with each holiday. In the light of marketing today, they were slow learners. It wasn't until after the World War II that advertising really caught on.

Why is it Americans can't keep their hands off Halloween? Women in particular love the untamed and the unexplained as well as Halloween's ever-popular pagan connections to the spirit world, which remain forever fascinating. Halloween provides something to look forward to. Halloween exists where we should all live, within an evolutionary process that continually recreates itself.

Hang on to your hat—it's a night for children of all ages to shine until they drop. It can also be one scary night if you want it to be. You can play god or you can play dead in the living room and scare your friends.

In reality it's not a holiday; it's a resurrection, an instant vacation from life. Never shall we be able to get a grip on Halloween, as we have on Christmas and Easter, because there is nothing to grab on to. Halloween is a transparent invasion of the mind. Thank heavens, because if it weren't, God forbid, it might become a legal holiday.

Halloween's greatest service to mankind was finding death "alive" and publicizing it. How comforting it is to realize that making the transition from one life to another is not a matter of distance, but a matter of desire.

Here is a letter, in part, written by an ancestor of mine:

> *...In years to come know this Sabbath is a night to remember from whom you have descended. Honor those who have come before you. Make pure your heart...still your body and empty your mind...Listen, listen...and Great Good Fortune shall come upon you this night...for they will speak to you...of what you need to know.*

> **—Ann Hopper, 1849**

I am reluctant to lay aside my pen, for this is but the beginning of a story without end...

We witches will be with you.

PART II

Halloween's Legacy

1

Ghost Tracking

Hunting for ghosts is a human curiosity, or perhaps it's a desire to get a closer look at death. Either way, it is a serious endeavor that can be a very rewarding experience on several levels. It's not a game. It's witnessing the paranormal, if you're lucky. The tracking part is easy. Confronting a ghost face to face is another matter.

Accidental encounters are about as rare as those that are well planned. What you want is to find places where there have been ongoing sightings over a long period of time. Do the research, and you will succeed. You need a well-planned itinerary along with names and addresses, not of the ghosts, of the homeowners or the caretakers. Even for cemeteries, you may need an appointment. Many are locked at dusk, and that's when you want to be there.

Ghost-searching in the United States, unless you have a friend with a haunted house, can be discouraging. We don't have a lot of ghosts here because everything is so new, unlike England, where everything is so old and ghosts are so prolific. In fact, 80 percent of all historic homes in England date back hundreds of years, and they're all haunted.

England has, by law, preserved its history, which is all the better for visual encounters. Ghosts are an English tradition, handed down from generation to generation. This is because there are many confused spirits that are unwilling to leave home. You will find a vast array of interesting and well-known ghosts from which to choose.

In Europe, and especially throughout Britain, the supernatural has never been fully understood, although it has been accepted for as long as it has been experienced…which is longer than anyone remembers. Perhaps it's too much of a good thing? There are those who think so. Many years ago, Oxford University decided to investigate extra-sensory perception and supernatural happenings. Was this necessary? Spirits had already been seen and heard. Let us hope that the unexplained continues to slip through the dissecting fingers of science.

Fortunately, countries with an abundance of hauntings have knowledgeable ghost tracking guides as well as bus tours to castles and historic homes. Both Scotland and Wales are well stocked with wandering spirits, fewer humans, and the most beautiful scenery.

We ghost hunters should always remember to have compassion for our "brothers in limbo" and the suffering of those human beings who've died but never stopped living. Among these pages are suggestions for successfully leaving earth life. Unless you wish to stay and wander aimlessly, follow them. It's important for us to do everything we can to help these spirits to move on. Exorcisms by priests are often successful.

What is it that binds these people so tightly to Earth? Sadly, they remain as they were in life, but minus flesh and blood. In bygone days, many families lived together their entire lives. At death, packing up happiness, let alone misery, is hard to do, especially for Royals, who continue to haunt in abundance. These are the ties that bind.

Ghosts are not alone. They are surrounded by many unseen spirits with whom to commune. Slowly but surely, most realize they must get on with the next phase of life and let the living get on with their lives. Rising "above it all" is a matter of desire not distance, as I've said before. Ghosts don't have far to go. Nevertheless, many stay here for hundreds of years, endlessly haunting.

Spirits appear to us in varying degrees of visibility, but I divide them into two categories: "thick ghosts" and "thin ghosts." Thin spirits are transparent, ethereal, and difficult to see with the naked eye. Indeed, some are never seen but often heard moaning, groaning, mumbling, or even playing musical instruments. Thick spirits, on the other hand, are the opposite. They appear to be almost human.

When my father was a boy, he entered his bedroom one evening and saw a well-dressed elderly lady standing in the corner. She smiled, but as he approached her, she turned away. He followed her. As she walked straight through the closed door, he walked straight into it. Although he claimed to be a non-believer, he never stopped retelling his strange experience. This is what I would call a thick ghost. To be reconstituted into visible form requires an enormous amount of ectoplasmic energy to manifest a fully developed human reproduction like this one. It's impossible for most spirits, let alone thin, shadowy ghosts who might never bother trying.

Aside from the deranged and lost souls, ghosts come in all varieties, good, bad, wise, mean, funny, annoying, and so on. Annoying ghosts are exactly that. They make noises, and they move things around to get attention or to hopefully be seen. They want us to know they exist, especially royal ghosts, who often believe they still rule over their land and their subjects as they did in life. It may be impossible for them to let go of the power they once had.

This leads us directly to the animals who think and feel as their human masters did. They can't let go! Dogs especially haunt the estate grounds where in life they romped through the fields and gardens. Life must have been paradise for the pets and their masters. No wonder animals also haunt. Who wouldn't want to return to paradise?

Dogs are not the only animals to haunt in this world. I have a friend whose horse died of old age. To her, it was like losing a child. She turned his stall into a shrine complete with his harness, saddle, and blankets. Even his trophies made their way from house to barn. Not only did she keep fresh hay in his stall, but fresh flowers as well.

About four or five years after the animal's death, on a warm summer evening, my friend was awakened by the faint sound of whinnying. She ignored it. She no longer kept horses, and assumed the sound came from the neighboring horse farm. After hearing it on several occasions, finally one night, she dragged herself out of bed and down to the barn. All was quiet. The whinnying had stopped. Slowly, she slid open the barn door. There he was: her beloved, Starbright. He was barely visible, but it was enough for her.

What I find baffling, whether human or animal, are those who come back to haunt, expecting nothing to have changed. Is it simply an overwhelming desire to re-experience the happiness and love they believe death took away? Whatever it is, they seem quite willing to spend eternity blind to everything except their own familiar surroundings. It makes us realize that there are times when understanding death can be more difficult than understanding life.

Not only are there humans searching for ghosts, but there are also "ghosts searchers" who never stop looking for what they left behind or for what they desperately wanted in life but never got. This brings us back to those aimless wonders with no place to go.

Last but not least, we cannot forget what I call the psychic ghosts, which is probably what they were in life. Often referred to as "soul protectors" or "warning ghosts," these spirits have the power to see the future and forewarn the living of accidents, death, and other disasters. These are spirits who see life before it happens.

Talking about ghosts clears a path to finding them. What you want to look for are "real" ghosts. The ones who keep ghost guides in business. "Real" ghosts are no different from others except they have a reputation for showing up regularly, at the right time and in the right place. Also, they seem oblivious to spectators. They don't get spooked by photographers. Those behind tripods are never noticed. Fear not, whatever you see, film it. With the right equipment, you may be very surprised with what "develops."

2

The Haunted Bookshelf

- *Where the Ghosts Are,* by Hans Holzer

- *A Wee Guide to the Haunted Castles of Scotland,* by Martin Coventry, 2002 paperback

- *The Complete Idiot's Guide to Ghosts and Hauntings in the United States,* by Tom Ogden, 1999

- *Hans Holzer's Travel Guide to Haunted Houses,* 1999

- *Britain's Haunted Heritage,* by John Brooks

- *The Good Ghost Guide,* by John Brooks

- *Haunt Hunters' Guide to Florida,* by Joyce Moore

- *Haunted Houses of California, a Ghostly Guide,* by Antoinette May and Sylvia Browne, 1993

- *Haunted Castles of Britain and Ireland,* Barnes & Noble, September 2003

3

Witch Wisdom

- To understand life, you need to understand the other side of it.

- Kindness is almost as important as love…which it leads to.

- Help someone. Help everyone. Help yourself.

- Don't leave it to heaven unless you are sure you can't do it.

- Evil can be seen and heard. Look and listen.

- The worse things get…the better they become.

- It is in high places where you find narrow-minded people.

- If you serve only yourself, disease will come upon you.

- Don't let your words exaggerate your accomplishments.

- How great is the distance between who you are, and who you want to be?

- Evil stems from ignorance.

- Don't decide how you should be treated by your relatives…consider how you should treat them.

- Help comes from the unseen side of life.

- If you're getting married, don't wait until you're at the altar to realize you're not sure.

- Take the same care of the Earth and the animals as you do the children.

- There is always a way to turn what you don't want into something you do.

- Being right is a reward in itself. Go about your chores.

- Solve all your problems while they are small…to avoid being faced with the impossible.

- A wise witch accepts anyone in need of help.

- If you can't change your life…change how you live it.

- Children should be seen, often heard, and always helped.

- Never give in to anger.

- Say yes…then wait for a path to clear.

- Intuition is a faint memory from another time…reuse it.

- The supernatural goes beyond wisdom.

- Each life brings you closer to eternal perfection.

- When in doubt, intuition may be your only sense of direction.

- Every path you take is the right one if you have the strength to make it so.

- Our soul is sacred so our body doesn't have to be.

- If you here voices…listen.

- Do not worry about the future until you get there.

- If you know how…do it.

- Character comes with experience.

- Those who fail to see the truth…follow those who do, without realizing it.

- There are only two kinds of great wealth…physical and mental.

- Obstacles are there to force us in another direction.

- Be thoughtful…not forceful. Be flexible…not rigid.

- When least expected, evil doers self-destruct.

- Justice is not a dream, it's a virtue.

4

Witch Tips

- Put your Halloween candles in the freezer a day before you plan to use them. They will last longer and drip less.

- Mix crispy chow mien noodles with nuts and chips in your holiday snack bowl. Yummy!

- If you plan to make a Halloween meatloaf for black cats, add cinnamon. They love it. So do witches.

- Want to keep gravy or sauces hot? If can't do it by magic, pour it into a thermos so it's ready when you are.

- If you drop an egg into a bowl of water and it rises to the top, there's an evil spirit in your house.

- Keep rice in an airtight container in the freezer. It will stay fresh forever.

- Flour keeps very well in a canister in the fridge for more than 2 years.

- Stir-fry vegetables in apple juice for a change. Great taste!

- Don't add oil to the water when cooking pasta. It keeps pasta from absorbing the sauce.

- On Halloween, plastic spiders are a nice holiday touch on everything from breakfast food to broccoli. Make sure young children know they are not to be eaten.

- Thin slice sweet potatoes. Brush with oil, sprinkle with paprika and cinnamon. If from the garden, bake at 425 degrees for 30 minutes. If from the can, fry the potatoes.

- When roasting a chicken, if you like crispy skin, <u>don't baste</u>.

- If you use bamboo skewers for grilling, before using, soak them in water for an hour so they won't burn.

- When making a carrot cake, use more carrots and more sugar than the recipe suggests.

- Keep lemons fresh longer in a large glass jar with "screw top." Fill it with water and put in the fridge.

- Use pretzel sticks instead of boring tooth picks for hors d'oeuvres, such as, cherry tomatoes, meatballs, stuffed olives, cheese balls, etc.

- Eat a few pieces of crystallized ginger every day. Incredibly healthy! It's a blood thinner, and it relieves arthritis and helps prevents strokes.

- Is your turkey bored with your cranberry sauce? Stir in a little sour cream and horseradish. Keep adding and tasting until you get it right.

- Don't use all that butter and syrup on hot pancakes. Sprinkle each one with powdered sugar instead. They glaze over to everyone's delight.

- My mother has a fetish about hot dinner plates. She puts them in an empty dishwasher on the "dry cycle" just before using.

- If you forget to tell the butcher to cut up the chicken, wash the garden shears. They are great cutting through bone.

- Can't lose weight? Eat three small healthy meals during the day. After 6 PM drink only water and eat nothing.

- Fill clear-plastic gloves with colored water and freeze to make ice "hands" that will float in your punch bowl.

- An ice cream scoop is good for scooping out pumpkins.

- Put dried flowers, brown leaves, and bare branches in a hollowed-out pumpkin with a few plastic creepy crawlers for a Halloween centerpiece.

- For trick-or-treaters consider non-edible, useful items like pencils, erasers, crayons, or small toys.

- Remember to put a black candle and a white candle on your table (not only for Halloween). The black candle is a magnet for good energy as the white candle burns off negativity.

- Make a scarecrow by stuffing a pair of jeans and a long-sleeved shirt with newspaper. Stuff a mask for its head. Add straw sticking out of the neck and the sleeves to make him look like he's stuffed with straw.

5

Witch Food

CREEPY CREPES
(Pancakes for busy witches)

- Whisk together about 2 cups of Bisquik, 1 egg and enough water to make a thin batter.

- Add about (witches never measure) 1/2 cup powdered cocoa and whisk.

- Add water to thin if necessary.

- Allow to stand 3 minutes and whisk again.

- Preheat buttered skillet on high and throw them on.

- Top with strawberries, whipped cream and chocolate syrup.

SPIDER SNACKERS
(For kids to make and eat)

Whole wheat bread (2 slices for each snacker)

Peanut butter

Jam (your choice)

Fried cheese curls (the thin, unhealthy kind)

Raisins

- Use scissors or a cookie cutter to make square bread <u>round.</u>

- Spread peanut butter on 1 round slice, jam on the other round.

- Insert 3 "spider legs" (cheese curls) into peanut butter with each set of legs opposite the other.

- Top with jam round.

- Insert raisins for the eyes.

- Do not refrigerate, cover with saran wrap until ready for use.

<u>BONFIRE CHICKEN</u>
(Old family recipe, greatly modernized)

1 whole chicken, 3 to 4 lbs.

1 jar orange marmalade

1 package of onion soup mix

- Combine soup mix and marmalade in large bowl.

- Cover chicken on all sides with marmalade.

- Put witches broom handle through center of chicken and rotate over bonfire for 20 minutes.

- If you prefer to use an oven, preheat at 350 degrees.

- Cook for one hour and fifteen minutes.

- It's done when leg can be moved up and down with ease.

WITCHY HASH BROWNS
(For potato lovers)

Large pkg. of frozen hash brown potatoes, thawed

8-oz. package shredded cheddar cheese

6 scallions or more coarsely chopped

1 cup sour cream

1 can cheddar cheese soup

- Combine all ingredients in large mixing bowl.

- Grease 13" x 9" inch baking dish.

- Spread mixture evenly in dish.

- Bake at 375 degrees for about 55 minutes.

Serves 8

IRISH JACK'S BEANS

Legend has it, Irish Jack cooked his beans in a clay pot over his "hot coals from Hell." I have added a few ingredients.

8 slices of bacon.

3/4 cup chopped onion

1/2 cup chopped green pepper

1/2 cup ketchup

1-1/2 teaspoons horseradish

2 cans of baked beans (remove pork)

- In a large skillet cook bacon until crisp, and drain.

- Pour off excess fat from skillet, leaving enough to sauté pepper and onion.

- Add ketchup and horseradish.

- Stir in beans and simmer for about 5 minutes.

- Set aside.

- Crumble bacon and stir into bean mixture.

Serves 4

APPLE HEAVEN
(Great-grandmother made this for Sunday breakfast.)

5 or 6 thick slices of stale Italian bread

1 stick of butter at room temperature

4 or 5 "golden delicious" apples

Sugar

- Butter baking dish and butter 1 side of each bread slice.

- With buttered side up, cover bottom of dish with slices.

- Peel apples and cut in thick slices.

- Place apples on top of bread and sprinkle with sugar.

- Top with the remaining apples and sprinkle with more sugar.

- Cut butter into pieces and dot generously over apples.

- Bake at 450 degrees for about 20 to 25 minutes or until caramelized or brown.

SOUL CAKES

For centuries these tiny cakes were given as gifts to the living and the dead on All Hallows Eve. Because "hallows" means "holy," a tiny cross or religious trinket was inserted in the center of each cake.

- Buy (or bake) cupcakes or muffins
- Cut a small "circle" in center of each cake about a 1-inch deep hole.
- Carefully remove circle and lay it aside.
- Insert trinket (wrapped or not) in the hole.
- Then place the "circle" back in cake.
- Top with jam or icing.

I save the "fortune" in fortune cookies to insert in the hole for special occasions. You can make up your own variations.

DEVIL'S BRUNCH

Butter

6 eggs

1/2 cup milk

1/2 medium onion chopped

1 teaspoon mustard

1/2 teaspoon curry powder

- Beat eggs with whisk.
- Add salt, pepper, milk, mustard, and curry powder.
- Fry chopped onion in butter over medium heat.
- Then add egg mixture to skillet.
- Scramble quickly. Eat slowly.

(Serve with The Devil's Own Fried Tomatoes.)

THE DEVIL'S OWN FRIED TOMATOES

1 tablespoon butter

2 large firm tomatoes

Cornmeal

- Cut tomatoes in thick slices.

- Sprinkle with salt, pepper, and garlic powder.

- Coat both sides of each slice with cornmeal.

- Melt butter in skillet.

- Brown on both sides and serve.

You'll Scream!

About the Author

Diana Millay is a veteran actor turned author. Her credits include Broadway shows, films, and more than 100 leading roles on television. She is well known for the TV series *Dark Shadows* and the cult-classic film *Tarzan and the Great River*. Diana is the author of the cookbook *I'd Rather Eat Than Act* and *How to Create Good Luck* on audiocassette.

Diana gives lectures and workshops extending from Creating Luck to Creative Living.

For more information, visit www.dianamillay.com.

0-595-29263-1

www.ingramcontent.com/pod-product-compliance
Lightning Source LLC
Chambersburg PA
CBHW031259280526
45784CB00004B/1918